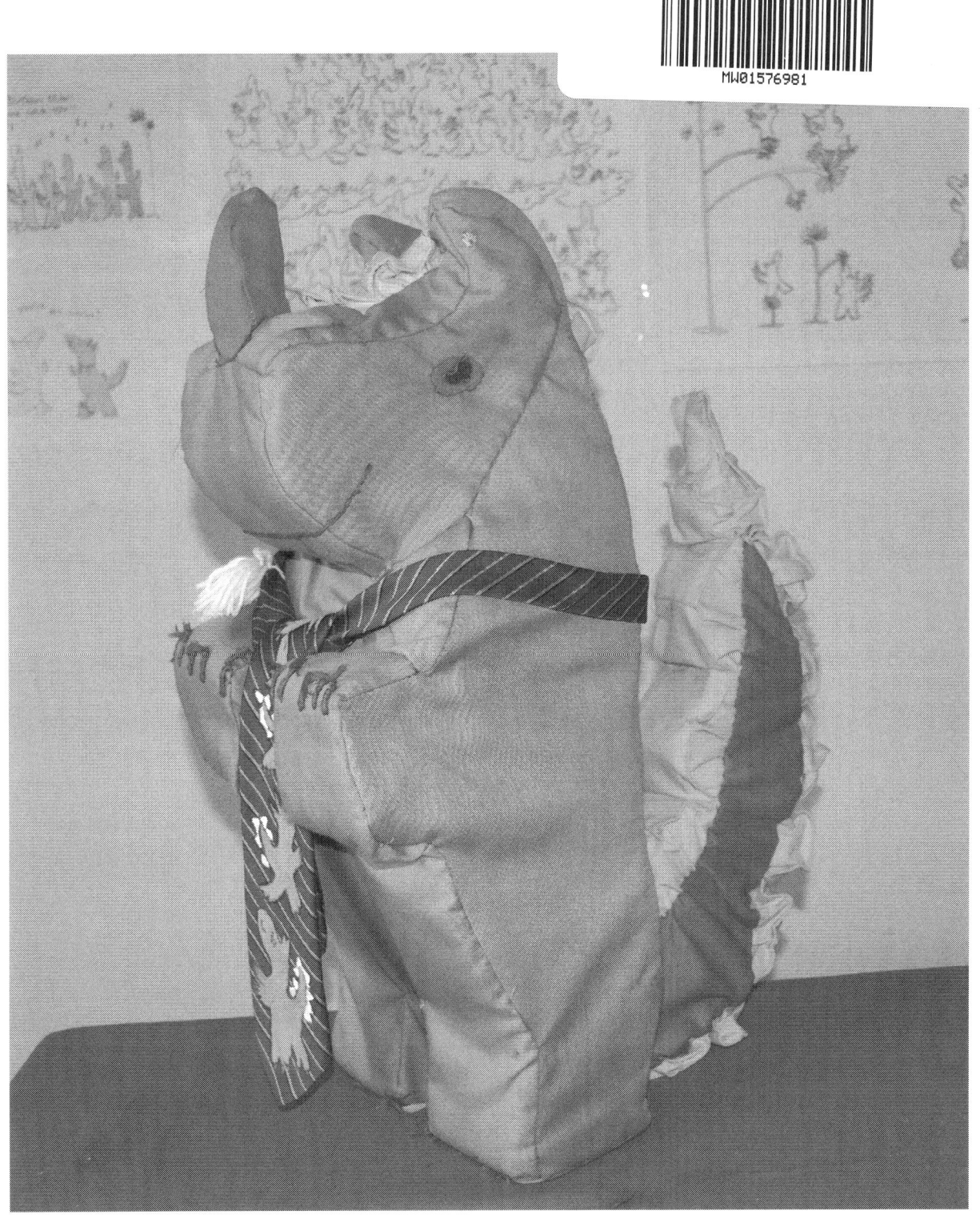

Introducing my lower case alphabet coloring book.

Welcome friends!

We invite you to take the time to look carefully at each individual in each letter. It's our experience that the dragons decide what letter they want to be part of and where they want to be placed!

Hope you enjoy this book.
I can be reached at:

Marian Brickner
insect1@att.net

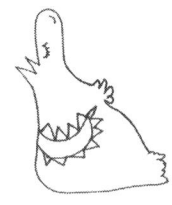

No part of this book may be reproduced in any form or by any electronic or mechanical means including photocopying, recording, or information storage and retrieval without permission from Marian Brickner and her Dragons.

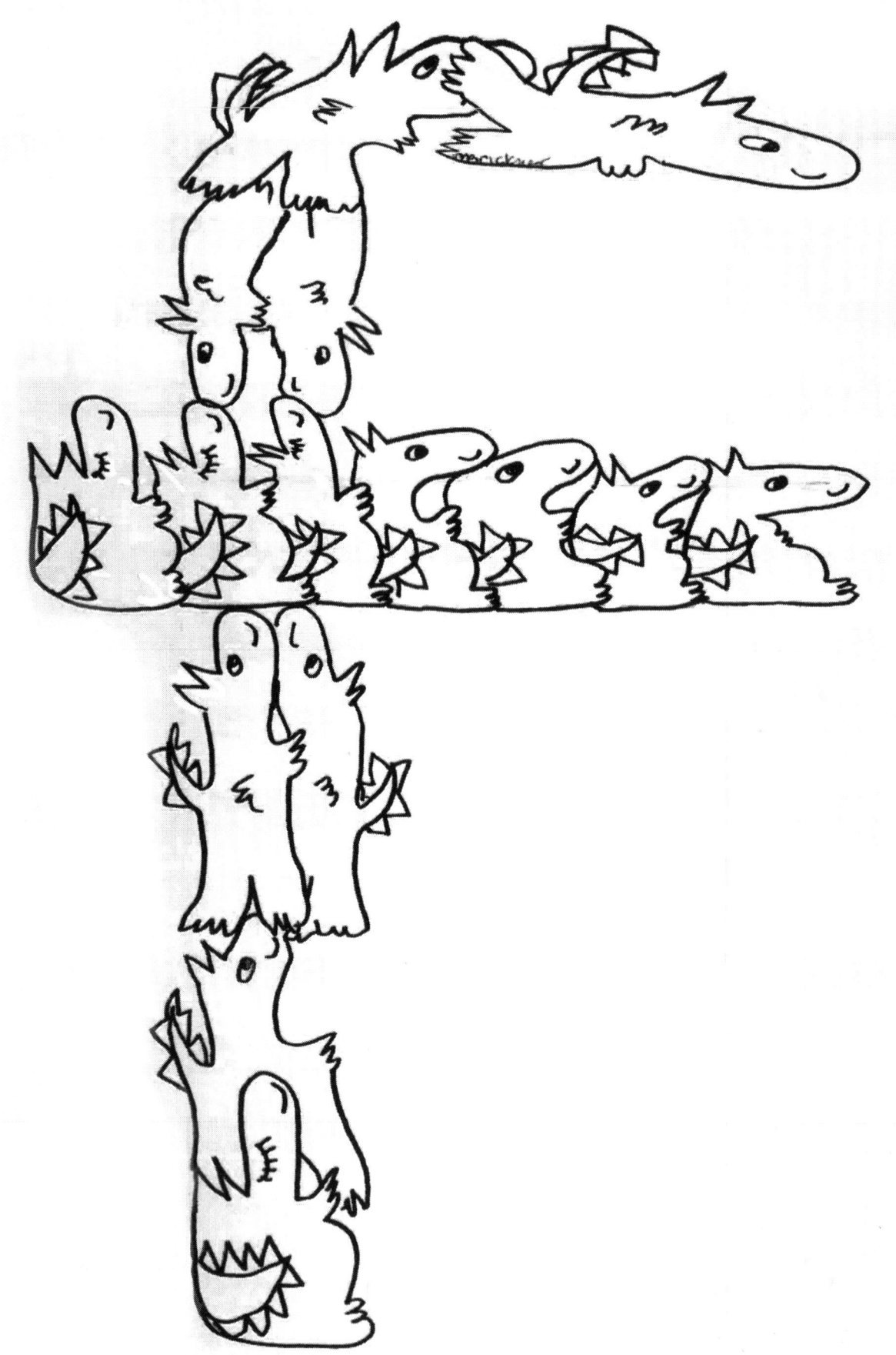

Marian Brickner

Marian Brickner

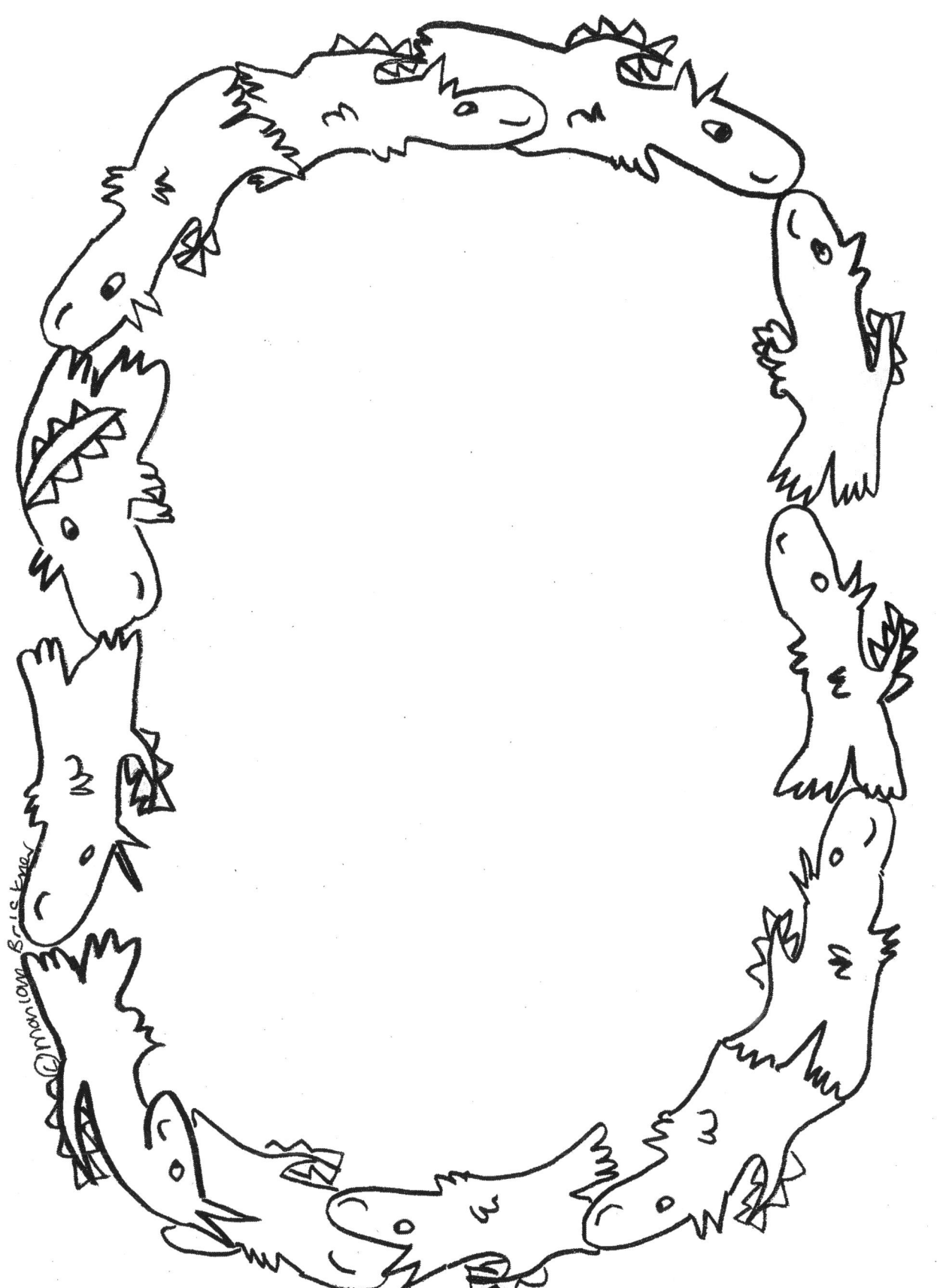

21

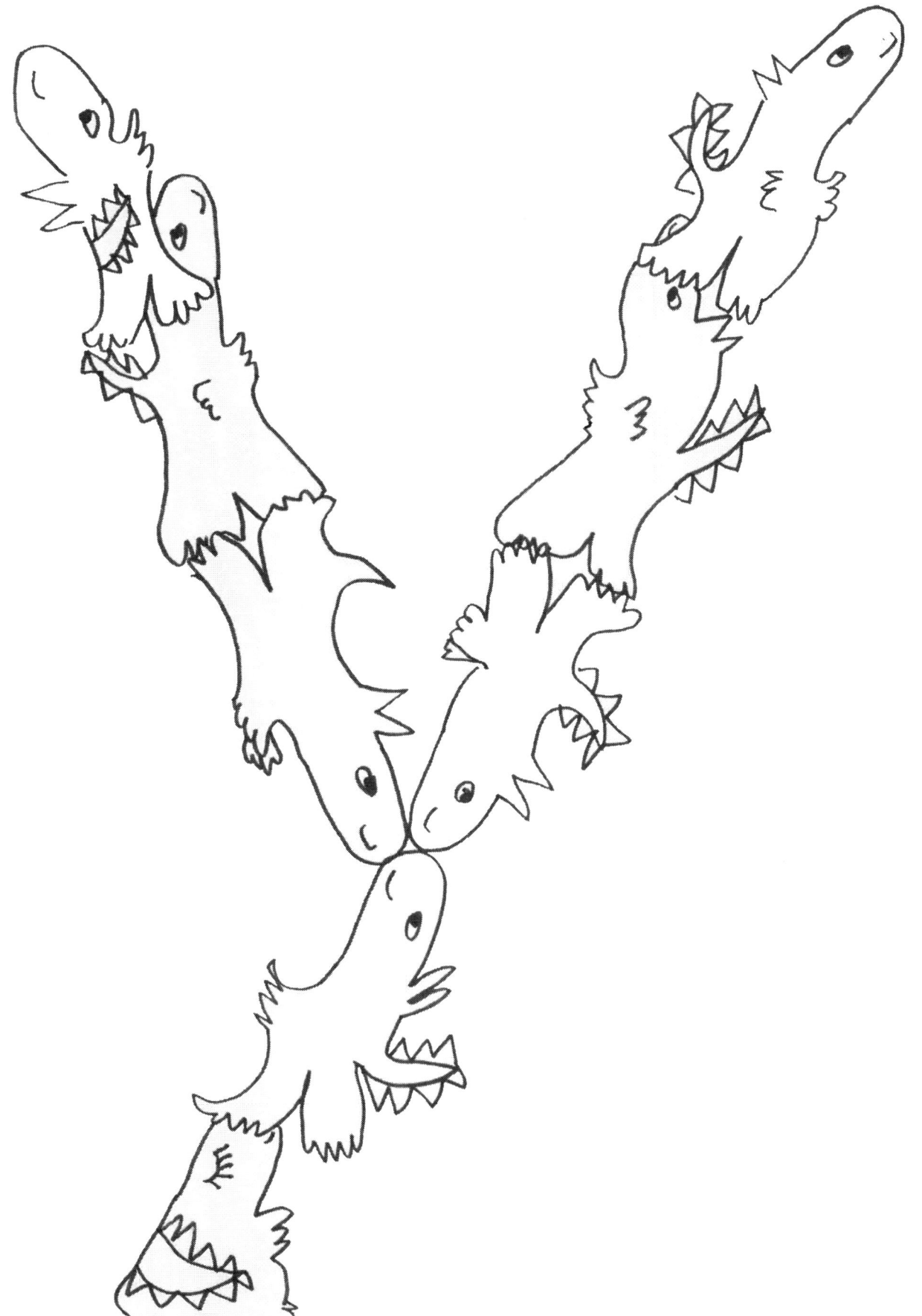

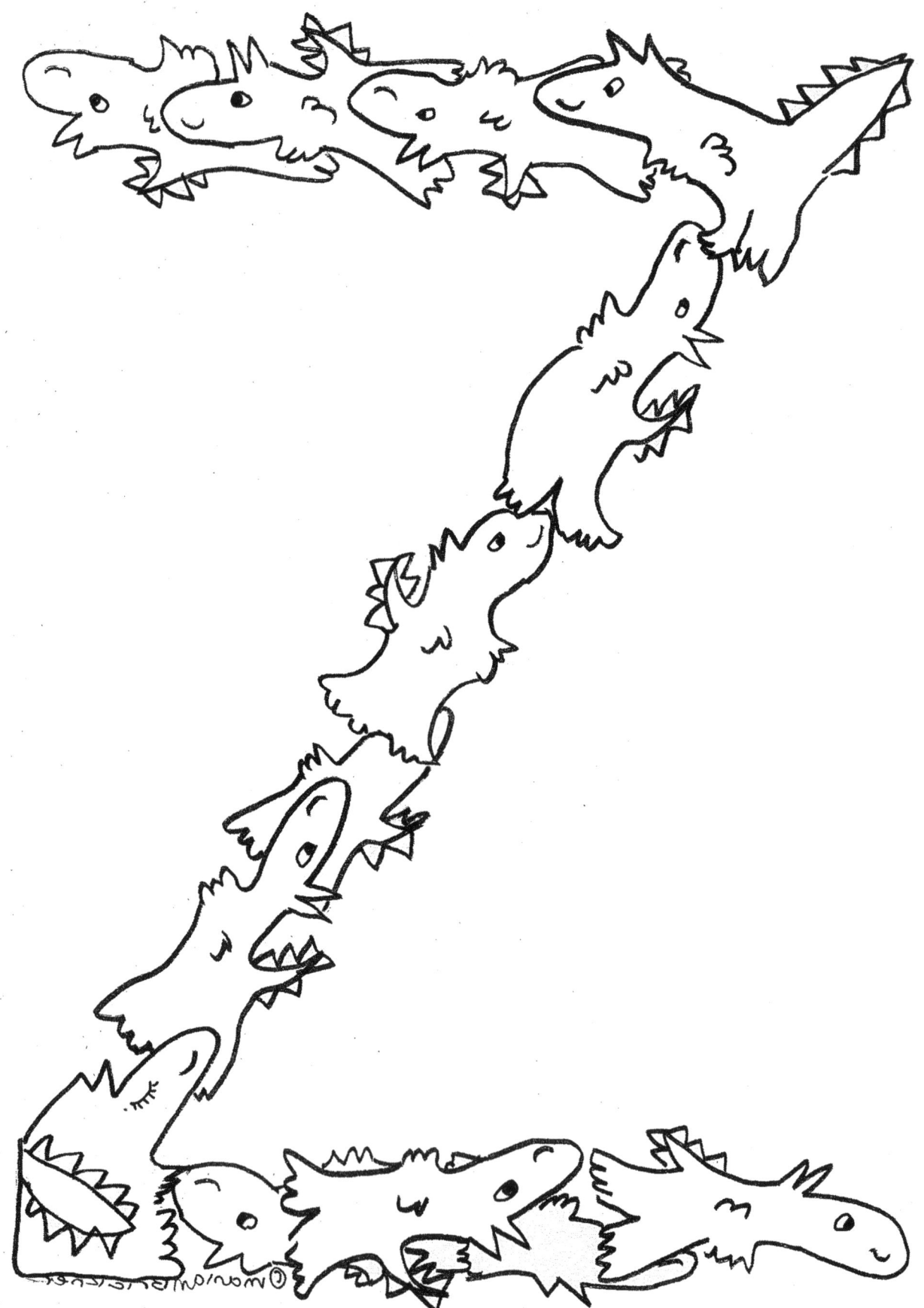

Books by Marian Brickner

Cat Books

Lexi My Cat
Cat Portraits
Cats
CATS SPEAK

Dog Books

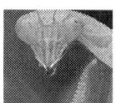

Barnhunt
Dogs of Circle Lake
Dog Portraits
With Bright Shiny Faces
Seasoned Dogs

Books for Fun
Go Fish!
What are they thinking?
What's a Family Anyway?
Mutts and Rascals
Animals Don't Wear Lipstick
Subliminal Nuances
of Animal Behavior

Bonobo Books

Lorel (mom age 35) and Lucy (age 1)

I'm Lucy, A Day in the Life
of a Young Bonobo
Is Lucy Singing?
Grooming Bonobos Lucy Loves It
Growing up Bonobo
Bonobo Lucy Grows up
Bonobo Lucy and her baby Yuli

Empathy Books
Insides out
You Scared me
I'm Different -You're Different

Coloring Books
Tra La La
Time to Smell the Flowers
A to Z Coloring book

Marian Brickner at
La Vallee des Singes in
Romagne, France

Initially known for photographing BONOBOS, (that's a picture of me in France where I was photographing Lucy), I have switched my attentions to using the DRAGON character to remind us that doing the impossible simply takes longer!
I have two websites,
www.marianbricknerphotography.com
and
marianbricknercartoons .com.

Would love to hear from you.

insect1@att.net

Made in the USA
Columbia, SC
17 January 2018